May you be blessed

by the POWER OF GOD,

today and always.

Sources: Cymbala, Jim with Dean Merrill. *Fresh Faith*.
Zondervan, 1999; *Fresh Power*, Zondervan, 2001; *Fresh Wind,
Fresh Fire*. Zondervan,1997. With Stephen Sorenson. *The Life
God Blesses*. Zondervan, 2001.

Requests for information should be addressed to:
Inspirio, The gift group of Zondervan
Grand Rapids, Michigan 49530
http://www.inspiriogifts.com

Published in association with the literary agency of Ann
Spangler & Associates, 1420 Pontiac Rd., S.E.
Grand Rapids, MI 49506

Compiler: Doris Rikkers
Associate Editor: Janice Jacobson
Product Manager: Tom Dean
Design: Lookout Design Group, Inc.

Printed in China
02 03 04/HK/ 4 3 21

THE
PROMISE
OF GOD'S
POWER

JIM CYMBALA

inspirio™

CONTENTS

Jesus said, "You will receive power when the Holy Spirit comes on you; and you will be my witnesses in Jerusalem, and in all Judea and Samaria, and to the ends of the earth."

— ACTS 1 : 8

GOD'S POWER CHANGES LIVES

If anyone is in Christ,

he is a new creation; the old

has gone, the new has come!

—2 CORINTHIANS 5:17

FROM PASTA
TO PREACHING

When Michael Durso opens his Bible to preach, you would never guess that he didn't come up the normal ministerial route. Raised in an Italian Catholic family, Michael was the first-born of three sons destined to inherit the family's gourmet pasta business. Everyone in the area knew that if you wanted the best, freshest linguine or mozzarella for your Sunday feast, Durso's on Utopia Parkway in Flushing was the place to get it.

Money was plentiful for the Durso family, and Michael showed an aptitude for making lots of it. The young man graduated from a Catholic high school and immediately went to work full-time in the family business. After a few years, he met a girl named Maria, who had inherited a fair amount of money herself. The two of them enjoyed the fast life of high-class drugs in the early seventies.

Michael was used to taking vacations to exotic resorts where drugs and immorality were the order of the day. One day, while at a resort in Mexico, Maria made an odd comment.

Recently she had been feeling vaguely empty, in spite of all their money and life of pleasure. She suggested that maybe when they returned to New York, they should go to church. She said that God seemed to be saying to her, *Give me your life.* Michael was mildly irritated. He frowned but said okay just to pacify her.

And that is how the young couple ended up at a Sunday night service in a gospel church in the Bay Ridge section of Brooklyn. Michael remembers being in a defiant mood. "I dressed as outrageously as I could, in a black form-fitting leather outfit, yellow boots, four earrings in one ear. I mainly wanted to shock these religious people. I was totally obnoxious."

And then ... the meeting was being brought to a close with an invitation to receive Christ. All at once, Michael turned sober. "Suddenly, I felt overwhelmed. I knew my life was headed for hell. All my confidence in my religious upbringing and my smart image vanished. I felt ashamed of my appearance. Both Maria and I headed for the front.

"People came around and began praying for us. Both of us started weeping. Soon the pastor approached us and did something very unusual: He anointed our foreheads with oil and then said, 'Lord, I pray that this couple will be used by you in the days and years ahead.' We were perplexed by that."

Before the end of the week, Michael had moved out of the apartment he and Maria shared to return to his parents' home until a legitimate wedding could be arranged.

In time Michael and Maria came to the Brooklyn Tabernacle and began to seek grounding in the Christian faith. We noticed in both of them a heart to follow God, to study his Word, and to give evidence of his grace and love. Michael and Maria got involved quickly. They organized a street ministry, taking groups from the choir and other workers to perform outdoor concerts in the summer. Whenever we needed help for a task, Michael was willing to take time off from work to pitch in.

Years went by, and in 1984 the board of a struggling church in Brooklyn offered to turn over their building to me if I would promise to oversee the work as long as I was alive. It was a wonderful gift from God, and our pastoral staff began to pray about how best to start a new church in this area. We all sensed the Spirit of God directing our attention to Michael and his wife to spearhead the new venture.

When I finally went over to Michael and Maria's house on a Friday night to say I felt that they should pastor this work, they could hardly believe what I was suggesting. This could mean eventually leaving the lucrative family business. And Michael didn't have the seminary training that ministers are expected to have.

But I believed in my heart that they had something vital: the anointing of the Holy Spirit and humble hearts to seek God's will.

Time has proven that this appointment was definitely what God wanted. We sent thirty or so of our members with Michael to help begin, and the little church grew and grew until it had to relocate. Today it meets in a converted theater and is one of the strongest lighthouses in our city, touching people for Christ in a powerful way.

JUST BE AVAILABLE

The Holy Spirit is still greater today than all our shortcomings and failures. He has come to free us from the restraints and complexes of insufficient talent, intelligence, or upbringing. He intends to do through us what only he can do. The issue is not our ability but rather our availability to the person of the Holy Spirit.

Every time we say, "I believe in the Holy Spirit," we mean that we believe that there is a living God able and willing to enter human personality and change it.

−J. B. PHILLIPS

God's divine power has given us everything
we need for life and godliness through
our knowledge of him who called us by
his own glory and goodness. Through these
he has given us his very great and precious
promises, so that through them you may
participate in the divine nature.

—2 PETER 1:3–4

God did not give us a spirit of timidity,
but a spirit of power, of love and
of self-discipline.

—2 TIMOTHY 1:7

I am not ashamed of the gospel,
because it is the power of God for the
salvation of everyone who believes.

—ROMANS 1:16

Dear Father,
please stir my heart
to reach out for all
that you
have promised me.
Forgive my dependence
on human resources
rather than on your power.
Teach me to pray and
wait upon you
in humility and faith;
send the wind and fire
of your Spirit upon me.
Transform me into
a person who bears
powerful witness
in word and deed
to the reality of
Jesus Christ our Savior.
I ask all of this
in his precious name.
Amen.

FROM DESPAIR TO JOY

One of the soloists in our choir is a woman in her mid-thirties named Robin Giles who grew up in Cleveland. When Robin was born to an unmarried twenty-one-year-old, it was obviously a "mistake." Her mother hated Robin's father and lived in a state of perpetual rage toward the daughter she was now stuck with.

From her early years Robin was yelled at, slapped about, and beaten. She never remembered a single hug or a kiss. Along the way, Robin's mother married an older man, a crane operator, whose presence helped to temper the eruptions in the home. But whenever the stepfather was gone, Robin feared for her life. More than once she was threatened with a gun. One day when she was nine and her mother began to berate her, the little girl fled to a large closet. When Robin peeked out to learn whether the storm had passed, she looked toward the kitchen—and saw her mother heating up a metal pancake turner over the gas range. Suddenly the woman turned and came flying in her direction. Robin ran for the safety of the closet again, but didn't get there in time. Soon the hot metal was searing itself against her arm. Her mother finally stopped the attack and began bandaging the wound. But still she snarled, "See what you made me do?!"

Robin was the opposite of an aggravating child. She made straight As in school, kept quiet, read a lot, and tried her best to please. But nothing could tame her mother's rage.

When Robin was twelve, her stepfather died of a heart attack, leaving her unprotected. When her mother caught her one summer night sitting on the front porch, talking to a boy who stood out on the sidewalk, she unleashed the most brutal beating to date—using a doubled-up electrical cord.

Robin ran away to a girlfriend's house, staying two weeks. But when she learned that a warrant had been issued for her arrest, she turned herself in with high hopes that the authorities would listen to her story and help her. To her shock, she was instead locked up in a juvenile detention center for three months. Bitterness began to grow inside her heart.

For Robin, the next eleven years were a rough road of self-doubt, depression, inner seething at the unfairness of life, irresponsible relationships and even a suicide attempt. Despite the help of a godly foster home during her high school years, "I had a chip on my shoulder," she admits. "I felt I had a right to be angry." Not until she was in her mid-twenties did a friend at work invite her to church, guiding her to a Savior who truly loved her and could be trusted. When she moved to New York a few years later, Robin's pastor in Cleveland recommended our church, and it has been our joy to have her here.

Robin is a walking example of Jesus' ability to set the captive free and to heal the broken-hearted. "God has taken the sting out of my past," she says. "For so long the memories of my mother's behavior kept me from experiencing abundant life.

But then I realized one day that the Lord had changed my heart toward her. I had hated her for so long. God totally took that away."

It is harder to repair this kind of damage to a person than to break the power of crack cocaine. Many would say Robin has every right to be bitter. What her mother did was absolutely dreadful. Robin Giles could have been a walking time bomb.

But God is stronger than any abuse. The Holy Spirit has the power to defuse the most raging resentment. He brings his power into the most troubled lives and produces something beautiful.

The LORD is close to the brokenhearted
and saves those who are crushed in spirit.

—PSALM 34:18

Do not grieve, for the joy of the LORD
is your strength.

—NEHEMIAH 8:10

The salvation of the righteous comes
from the LORD; he is their stronghold
in time of trouble.
The LORD helps them and delivers them;
he delivers them from the wicked and
saves them, because they take refuge in him.

—PSALM 37:39–40

I believe, and am growing more into this belief, that divine, miraculous, creative power resides in the Holy Spirit. If we look to the spirit of God and expect it to come from Him and Him alone then we shall honor the Spirit, and the Spirit will do His work.

I cannot help but believe that there are many Christians who want to be more efficient in the Lord's service. It is from the Holy Spirit that we may expect this power.

— D . L .   M O O D Y

Only the grace of God can teach us to say, "No!" properly and effectively.

All the human resolve we can muster and all the well-intentioned promises we can make are utterly powerless against the strength of fleshly desires. It is only as God's spirit works within us "to will and to act according to his good purpose" (Philippians 2:13) that we can experience daily victory over every besetting sin.

So God's heart of mercy provides for us
not only pardon from sin but also a daily
provision of spiritual food to strengthen us.

FATHER, I BRING ALL MY
FAILURES TO YOU IN JESUS'
NAME. I HAVE TRIED SO
HARD AND SO OFTEN TO
CHANGE. BUT MY PROBLEMS
ARE TOO BIG FOR ME TO
HANDLE. TODAY, I GIVE UP
AND THROW MYSELF TOTALLY
ON YOUR LOVE AND MERCY.
CLEANSE ME AND CHANGE
ME FROM THE INSIDE OUT.
TEACH ME HOW TO IMITATE
YOU — TO HAVE YOUR HEART
OF KINDNESS AND MERCY.
TEACH ME TO WALK IN THE
SPIRIT EVERY DAY SO I CAN
KNOW YOUR POWER AND
VICTORY. I REST IN YOUR
MERCY AND FAITHFULNESS.
AMEN.

SUPERNATURALLY
EMPOWERED

When the day of Pentecost came,
[the disciples] were all together in one place.
Suddenly a sound like the blowing of a violent
wind came from heaven and filled the whole
house where they were sitting. They saw
what seemed to be tongues of fire that
separated and came to rest on each of them.
All of them were filled with the Holy Spirit
and began to speak in other tongues as the
Spirit enabled them.

— ACTS 2:1-4

What God did on the Day of Pentecost was
dramatic and powerful. God by his Spirit
enabled ordinary men and women to do and say
things beyond their natural abilities. They
became supernaturally empowered. There was
no human explanation for what was taking place.

This is the story, in one way or another, of
every man, woman, or church that has ever been

used in great ways for God's glory. They were set on fire by God and that experience affected the world around them.

Praise God for his ability to lift us above ourselves! Otherwise, where would all of us be? Especially people such as my wife, Carol, and me, who never got to go to a Bible college or seminary … and others who say, "I don't have this talent or that ability." We can take courage from the fact that Jesus called fishermen to be his disciples—"losers" by the world's standards—but their lives were invaded by God and raised to amazing places.

The same tongues that had engaged in petty argument about who was the greatest, the same tongues that had denied the Lord and the fact of his resurrection were now overtaken by heaven itself.

In fact, sending his Holy Spirit to fill us is God's ordained way of equipping us, because it leaves little doubt about who should get all the glory. If our human intellect and abilities and talents produced the results, we could strut around saying, "My, we're pretty special, don't you think?" But men and women who are truly used by God are necessarily humbled because they know the true source of their strength.

When God moves into our lives,

*no obstacle
can stop him.*

In the last days, God says,
I will pour out my Spirit on all people.
Your sons and daughters will prophesy,
your young men will see visions,
your old men will dream dreams.
Even on my servants, both men and women,
I will pour out my Spirit in those days,
and they will prophesy.

—ACTS 2:17–18

The mind of sinful man is death,
but the mind controlled by the Spirit is life
and peace . . . You . . . are controlled
not by the sinful nature but by the Spirit,
if the Spirit of God lives in you.

—ROMANS 8:6,9

A POWERFUL
DIFFERENCE

The power to be different comes from heaven, not from our own strength. The Holy Spirit was given, as his name implies, so that we can live a holy life for God. Any other source or system, no matter how religious-sounding, is a fraud and leads to defeat because of the fleshly impulses of our sinful nature. The Holy Spirit's power is not an *option* for those who desperately want to be like Christ; he is the only answer. We must be delivered from the idea that Christianity begins with a supernatural new birth, sin is erased, the conscience is cleansed—but then it's up to us to try real hard to be good and obey God's commands. No, it is God's work from beginning to end. Just as forgiveness can *only* come through Christ's work on Calvary, daily living for the Lord can *only* be done through the Spirit.

CHANGED FROM THE INSIDE OUT

The summer of 1977 in New York City was open season for a crazed gunman who shot young women and then wrote sick letters to the newspapers. He said he was getting his orders to kill from a dog, and the entire city was terrified. What kind of fiend was this, we wondered, randomly shooting young women for no apparent reason?

After thirteen months the case on this nationally known, nationally feared criminal called "Son of Sam," was finally solved. David Berkowitz, a twenty-four-year-old postal worker living in Yonkers, a suburb just north of the city, was arrested. When taken to court, David openly pleaded guilty to killing five women and one man as well as wounding many others. Only New York State's ban on the death penalty kept him alive. His prison sentence ran to hundreds of years, and he was shipped off to Attica.

I gradually forgot about him until a few years ago when a woman I didn't know called the church office. She put me in touch with David, who had become a believer and trusted me. We developed a telephone friendship and exchanged letters. Gradually I heard about his early life, how he had grown up in the Bronx as an adopted child in a Jewish home.

"I was troubled psychologically and emotionally from early on," David told me, "and I proved to be a real handful for my parents. I felt somehow drawn to evil and occult things. It seemed that even as a child I was marked and cultivated by Satan for evil purposes." School was nothing but one problem after another. Since his mother was a practicing Jew, Gentile kids taunted David with anti-Semitic remarks, but he didn't really identify with any religion. The name of Jesus meant nothing specific to him.

After high school and three years in the army, David was vulnerable, and his emptiness of soul drew him to people and things that were increasingly dark.

The satanic group he joined was bent on creating mayhem. David began hauling big rocks onto overpasses and tossing them into the traffic below just to watch the accidents that would result. He started setting fires of all kinds—2,000 of them, which he carefully logged in a journal. In time David began picking off young women with a .44-caliber handgun on dimly lit streets and in lovers' lanes with their boyfriends.

In 1987 David was moved to Sullivan Correctional Facility. One night a young prisoner named Ricky Lopez approached him in the exercise yard. "He said that Jesus loved me and had a purpose for my life." Ricky kept walking alongside David day after day, becoming his friend. One day he presented him with a small New Testament with Psalms and suggested that he start reading the Psalms.

The Word of God penetrated David's heart. He soon knelt by his bunk and asked Jesus Christ to be his Savior and Lord. He wept as he laid aside the tremendous condemnation he felt for what he had done, which was weighing upon him all the more heavily now.

The Word was working on him, and he cried out for mercy.

Over the past decade and more, David has progressed in his faith. He is a diligent student of God's Word, and is now the chaplain's assistant at Sullivan. He has coordinated several concerts for the choir at the prison and says that the prison is his God-ordained sphere of ministry. "There's plenty to do here," David says, "but it's dangerous as well. God has warned me many times when something was about to *go down*."

David has become a dear friend to Carol and me. Not only that, he is also my brother in Christ, for God has changed the very "chief of sinners" — a demon-controlled serial killer — into a precious child of God. The strongest satanic chains have been broken by the Lord Jesus Christ.

The Holy Spirit can overcome hostile environments and fill us again and again with joy. He helps us swim against the strongest tide.

You are strong, and the word of God lives in you, and you have overcome the evil one.

— 1 JOHN 2:14

*Most people plot and plan themselves
into mediocrity, while now and again
somebody forgets himself into greatness.*

—E. STANLEY JONES

We who with unveiled faces all reflect the
Lord's glory, are being transformed into his
likeness with ever-increasing glory, which comes
from the Lord, who is the Spirit.

— 2 CORINTHIANS 3:18

Those who live in accordance with the Spirit
have their minds set on what the Spirit desires.

— ROMANS 8:5

Do not conform any longer to the pattern
of this world, but be transformed by the
renewing of your mind. Then you will be able
to test and approve what God's will is —
his good, pleasing and perfect will.

— ROMANS 12:2

LIVING EVIDENCE

On more than one occasion, Pam Pena—
the wife of one of our associate pastors—has
shared how the Lord delivered her from a
terrible eating disorder. Raised in a church-
going home in the New Jersey suburbs, she
was an emotionally needy teenager who
lacked self-confidence and felt worthless.
To please her friends, she began cutting
school, drinking and smoking. At age sixteen
she found herself pregnant. Her boyfriend
rejected her, and she was devastated. Feeling
all alone, she quickly obtained an abortion.

In the aftermath of this she told herself,
*Maybe if I turn to God and try harder to do
the right thing, he will accept me.* She didn't
realize that she was now trying to win God's
approval through her own efforts. As time
went on, these efforts left her empty.
She remained insecure about who she was
and became obsessed with the weight she
had gained.

In her first two years at a Christian
college, Pam engaged in compulsive dieting
and vigorous exercise. By the end of her
sophomore year she was weak and thin from

bingeing and purging up to five times a day. She dropped out of college, went home and then fled to a secular college where her life spun further out of control. Someone introduced her to cocaine and she quickly became addicted. The next three years were a downward spiral of food abuse compounded by cocaine.

At a party one New Year's Eve, she went into the host family's bathroom and cleaned out the medicine chest of every pill she could find. At home the next day, she swallowed them and then lay down to die. While waiting she called a college friend—and that fortunately led to her rescue. But even six weeks in a treatment program couldn't break her compulsion over food.

In about a year, Pam attempted suicide a second time. She deliberately drove onto a major highway with her eyes closed and was hit by a bus. All during these turbulent years, her parents and their church family were earnestly praying that God would somehow rescue Pam from herself.

One morning while driving to work, Pam began to cry out to the Lord. Sobbing so hard that no sound would come from her throat, her soul nevertheless was shouting, O God, *I want to live!*

"The love of God came into the car," she remembers. "I finally gave up trying to be loved by people. I quit striving for approval. I saw my self-deception. Finally I saw with my spiritual eyes what I had been missing. I seemed to fall into God's arms, saying, 'I give up. I *will* believe that you love me.'"

Pam never touched cocaine again. She stopped smoking cigarettes within weeks. And God the Holy Spirit went to work on her eating disorder. Over the next two years, without any psychotherapy or seminars, Pam gradually stopped the harmful behavior. When difficult moments came during the process, God seemed to assure her that he had her by the hand and would pull her completely from the pit where she had lived for so long.

"I had to trust the Lord that if I ate food and kept it down, I wouldn't gain weight—or if I did, he would enable me to deal with that situation. Little by little the Holy Spirit taught me how to eat."

Pam often tells about one particular mealtime, Thanksgiving 1988. Holidays can be the worst nightmare for a bulimic person. "I sat down at the big table with all the other relatives, had Thanksgiving dinner—and even accepted some dessert. As I was eating it, the Holy Spirit seemed to whisper in my ear, *You're fine. It's finally over.*"

The fact is that God performed a miracle in the life of Pam Pena. Today she is a wonderful servant of the Lord who brings others to freedom in our church. She was healed, not through human strategies, but rather through the gracious influence of the Holy Spirit.

LORD, I BRING MY BURDENS
AND HEARTACHES TO YOU AT
THE THRONE OF GRACE.
YOU HAVE PROMISED TO HELP
ME IN MY TIME OF TROUBLE
AND NEED. I REST UPON YOUR
WORD AND CAST EVERY ONE
OF MY CARES UPON YOU.
WORK ON MY BEHALF SO THAT
OTHERS MIGHT KNOW THE
AWESOMENESS OF YOUR POWER
AND THE FAITHFULNESS OF
YOUR LOVE. IN CHRIST'S NAME,
AMEN.

May the God of hope fill you with

all joy and peace as you trust in him,

so that you may overflow with hope by the

power of the Holy Spirit.

— R O M A N S   1 5 : 1 3

GOD'S POWER TURNS DEFEAT INTO VICTORY

I waited patiently for the Lord;
 he turned to me and heard my cry.
He lifted me out of the slimy pit,
 out of the mud and mire;
 he set my feet on a rock
 and gave me a firm place to stand.
He put a new song in my mouth,
 a hymn of praise to our God.

—PSALM 40:1–3

God will be faithful to see you through

your storm and time of difficulty.

Don't look down in discouragement,

but look up to him, who has promised

to stay with you even "through the

valley of the shadow of death"

(Psalm 23:4). Did the Lord begin this

beautiful work of grace in your life

only to let you fall into some black hole

of hopelessness and despair? Never!

O LORD my God, I called to you for help

and you healed me.

O LORD ... you spared me from going

down into the pit.

Sing to the LORD, you saints of his;

praise his holy name.

—PSALM 30:2–4

UNFORESEEN FRUIT

In 1921, a missionary couple named
David and Svea Flood went from Sweden to
the heart of Africa with another couple, the
Ericksons. Both couples felt led by the Lord to
take the gospel to a remote area. At the village
of N'dolera they were rebuffed by the chief,
so they decided to go half a mile up the slope
of a nearby mountain and build their own
mud huts.

The missionaries prayed for a spiritual
breakthrough, but there was none. The only
contact they had with the villagers was a young
boy, who was allowed to sell them chickens and
eggs twice a week. Svea Flood decided that
even if this was the only African she could talk
to, she would still try to lead the boy to Jesus.
And in fact she succeeded.
But the missionaries received
no other encouragements.

When malaria struck
the group, the Ericksons
returned to the central
mission station. David and
Svea Flood remained. Soon
Svea discovered that she was

pregnant. A little girl was born, whom they named Aina, but Svea died seventeen days later.

David Flood snapped. He buried his wife, then took his child back to the mission station. Giving his newborn daughter to the Ericksons, he snarled, "I'm going back to Sweden. God has ruined my life."

Eight months later, both of the Ericksons died within days of each other. The baby was turned over to some American missionaries who adjusted her name to "Aggie" and brought her back to the United States. Aggie grew up in South Dakota, attended a Bible college and met and married Dewey Hurst, who became the president of a Christian college in the Seattle area.

One day a Swedish religious magazine appeared in Aggie's mailbox. There in a photograph of a primitive setting was a grave with a white cross—and on the cross were the words SVEA FLOOD. A college faculty member translated the article: it was about missionaries who had come to N'dolera long ago, the birth of a white baby, the death of the young mother, the one little African boy who had been led to Christ, and how, after the whites had all left, the boy had grown up and finally persuaded

the chief to let him build a school in the village.

Gradually he won all his students to Christ, the children led their parents to Christ and even the chief became a Christian. Today there were six hundred Christian believers in that one village, all because of the sacrifice of David and Svea Flood.

For the Hursts' twenty-fifth wedding anniversary, the college presented them with the gift of a vacation to Sweden. There Aggie sought to find her real father. An old man now, David Flood was still bitter. He had one rule in his family: "Never mention the name of God—because God took everything from me."

Taking her father gently in her arms, Aggie said, "Papa, I've got a little story to tell you, and it's a true one. You didn't go to Africa in vain. Mama didn't die in vain. The little boy you won to the Lord grew up to win that whole village to Jesus Christ. The one seed you planted just kept growing and growing.

Today there are six hundred African people serving the Lord because you were faithful to the call of God in your life...."

"Papa, Jesus loves you. He has never hated you."

The old man turned back to look into his daughter's eyes. His body relaxed. He began to talk. And by the end of the afternoon, he had come back to the God he had resented for so many decades.

Svea Flood gave her all, not counting the cost and not expecting to be rescued before pain and suffering would strike. She died far too young by human standards. And yet her accomplishments in the spiritual realm are beyond measuring.

Jesus said, "I tell you the truth,

unless a kernel of wheat falls

to the ground and dies,

it remains only a single seed.

But if it dies,

it produces many seeds. ...

Whoever loses his life

for my sake will find it."

–JOHN 12:24;
MATTHEW 10:39

FOOLISH TOOLS

In the familiar story of David and Goliath, there is a wonderful moment when the giant gets irked at the sight of his young opponent. "Am I a dog, that you come at me with sticks?" he roars (1 Samuel 17:43). Goliath is genuinely insulted. "Come here ... and I'll give your flesh to the birds of the air and the beasts of the field!" (v. 44)

Does David flinch? Does he decide to make a strategic retreat behind some tree or boulder, thinking maybe to buy a little time?

Absolutely not.

"As the Philistine moved closer to attack him, *David ran quickly toward the battle line to meet him*" (v. 48, emphasis added).

That is the picture of what God wants for us today: *running toward the fray!*

David's weaponry was ridiculous, a sling and five stones. It didn't matter. God still uses foolish tools in the hands of weak people to build his kingdom. Backed by prayer and his power, we can accomplish the unthinkable.

When we get serious about

drawing upon God's power,

remarkable things will happen.

Jesus said, "My grace is sufficient for you,
for my power is made perfect in weakness."

–2 CORINTHIANS 12:9

Do not be afraid. Stand firm
and you will see the deliverance the LORD
will bring you today. ... The LORD will fight
for you; you need only to be still.

–EXODUS 14:13–14

Jesus said, "In this world you
will have trouble. But take heart!
I have overcome the world."

–JOHN 16:33

The only power that will keep us victorious on a daily basis comes through the Holy Spirit. It's not about what we can do, but what God can do!

BACK FROM THE "DEAD"

Roberta Langella was born in Brooklyn, the fourth of six children, and was raised on Staten Island. Her father was a longshoreman who provided a good living and a Catholic education for all his children. Roberta was happy to be part of what she thought was a stable, loving home.

But when she was only eleven, her family moved to Florida to be near her mother's parents. The only trouble was, her dad didn't come with them. Her parents soon divorced. She couldn't believe what was happening. Her family had always stuck together. She felt that if she couldn't rely on grown-ups to do the right thing, what was life all about anyway? She was shattered.

Within a year or two, Roberta was acting out her unhappiness by drinking and smoking pot. Her mom remarried, which only made matters worse. Roberta and her new stepfather fought all the time. At age sixteen Roberta went back to New York to live with her dad for a year. Then she dropped out of school and took off to crisscross the country on her own.

A year later, back in New York, Roberta was living with a man twice her age. She just wanted somebody—anybody—to love her and take care of her. Unfortunately this guy was an IV drug abuser. Before long, they were both on cocaine and then heroin. Roberta ended up overdosing several times. One night she took so many drugs her heart stopped beating. By God's grace someone discovered her and the paramedics revived her. She felt so bad about herself that she was sure nobody thought she was worth anything. This attitude led to one destructive relationship after another. An abusive boyfriend beat her so badly he broke her eardrum. Most of her other boy-friends were drug addicts, one was a dealer. She worked as a bartender in nightclubs, totally getting into the punk culture of the eighties that featured the "dead look." She frequented "shooting galleries" where twenty or thirty people got high all at once, sharing needles.

One early morning on her way home, Roberta walked past a sidewalk full of people waiting to get into the Brooklyn Tabernacle. All their happy faces made her angry! Back at home, she could hear the choir singing from her bedroom window and something in the music would touch her even though she didn't want to be touched. But she wouldn't go inside the church. She was sure Jesus could never love someone as strung out as she was.

Before long, she moved to the Upper West Side of Manhattan. One day she overheard her neighbor singing. When she asked about the songs, her neighbor told her they were what the choir sang at the Brooklyn Tabernacle. Roberta had moved away, but the church kept moving in on her.

Meanwhile, Roberta's drug and alcohol abuse intensified. She moved to Florida to be with her mother and went clean with the help of Narcotics Anonymous. But her newfound confidence came crashing down all too soon when a doctor unveiled a horrible fact—she was HIV positive.

After all the needle-sharing she had done over the years, she wasn't surprised, but she was mad at herself and at God. Back in New York, Roberta started her own business. Her brother Stephen encouraged her to come with him to the Brooklyn Tabernacle. Finally she agreed, but the old feelings of embarrassment and shame rose up again. She wanted the rush of drugs more than she wanted to keep struggling with life alone. After two years of living clean, she lapsed back into the world of crack cocaine.

Finally Roberta hit bottom at the end of a five or six-day crack binge. It was a Tuesday night when she ran out of money. For some reason she drove to the church and found herself at the altar shedding tears she couldn't stop. "Oh, God," she cried, "I need you in my life. Help me, please!" It was the moment of final surrender. From that point on, Roberta began to believe that God loved her. And with this newfound faith came hope and a slowly growing confidence.

Roberta Langella gave birth to a ministry called "New Beginnings," a weekly outreach to drug abusers and the homeless. She recruited fervent workers, who rode the subway every Sunday afternoon to the shelters and rehab centers to escort people to our church for a meal and the evening meeting. The love of the Lord just exudes from her life.

Roberta is a real trooper these days, even when she doesn't feel well. There's nobody too dirty, or too far-gone for her to care about. She sees herself in them. She is a living example of the power of God to pick up the downtrodden, the self-loathing, the addicted, and redeem them for his glory.

God has rescued us from
the dominion of darkness and brought
us into the kingdom of the Son
he loves, in whom we have redemption,
the forgiveness of sins.

—COLOSSIANS 1:13–14

The Holy Spirit has a way of short-circuiting human problems. Indeed, in exactly the same way as Jesus Christ in the flesh cut right through the matted layers of tradition and exposed the real issue; so we find the Spirit of Jesus dealing not so much with problems as with people. Since God's Holy Spirit cannot conceivably have changed one iota through the centuries, He is perfectly prepared to short-circuit, by an inflow of love, wisdom and understanding, many human problems today.

—J.B. PHILLIPS

You have taken off your old self
with its practices and have put on
the new self, which is being renewed in
knowledge in the image of its Creator.

—COLOSSIANS 3:9–10

Jesus said, "I am the resurrection
and the life. He who believes in me
will live, even though he dies;
and whoever lives and believes in me
will never die."

—JOHN 11:25–26

The gift of God is eternal life
in Christ Jesus our LORD.

—ROMANS 6:23

MAKE ROOM FOR GOD'S POWER

When it comes to spiritual matters, you and I will never know our potential under God until we step out and take risks on the front line of battle. We will never see what power and anointing are possible until we bond with our King and go out in his name to establish his kingdom. Sitting safely in the shelter of Bible discussions among ourselves, or complaining to one another about the horrible state of today's society, does nothing to unleash the power of God. He meets us in the moment of battle. He energizes us when there is an enemy to be pushed back.

When I was at my lowest, confounded by obstacles, bewildered by the darkness that surrounded us, unable even to continue preaching, I discovered an astonishing truth: God is attracted to weakness. He can't resist those who humbly and honestly admit how desperately they need him. Our weakness, in fact, makes room for his power.

If Israel followed the pillar
of fire and cloud
so carefully, how much more
should we the Holy Spirit.

—FRANK BARTLEMAN

God is waiting to empower us. The need today to confront the works of darkness are greater than they have ever been. The influence of filth and violence in people's lives will not be destroyed by polite talk. There is a divine antidote to the demonic powers that stir up young people to shoot up schools and worship dark impulses. Our only hope is in the power of the Holy Spirit. We have a mission from Jesus himself, and only the outpouring of the Spirit's power will enable us to make a difference.

Without the Spirit of God
we can do nothing.
We are as ships without wind
or chariots without horses.
Like branches without sap,
we are withered. Like coals
without fire, we are useless.

—CHARLES SPURGEON

FILLED WITH
THE SPIRIT

Dwight L. Moody never had the formal credentials to be ordained. That is why he was always called simply "Mr. Moody." He was short, stocky, and not particularly attractive in appearance. He mispronounced words regularly. If you read his personal letters, you will see all kinds of punctuation and spelling errors. Yet he addressed more people and brought more of them to Christ than anyone else in the nineteenth century. How did that happen?

A major spiritual turning point occurred in Moody's life that set him on the road to ministry. It was something that happened just across the East River from the borough of Brooklyn where our church is located—while he was walking on Wall Street no less! In late 1871, just a few weeks after the great Chicago fire, the thirty-four-year-old Moody had come east to try to raise money to rebuild the buildings he had lost. But, he writes, "my heart was not in the work of begging. I could not appeal.

I was crying all the time that God would fill me with His Spirit. Well one day, in the city of New York — oh, what a day! — I cannot describe it. I seldom refer to it; it is almost too sacred an experience to name. I can only say that God revealed Himself to me and I had such an experience of His love that I had to ask Him to stay His hand."

Oh, that all of us might receive, like Mr. Moody, something fresh from the Holy Spirit that revolutionizes our spiritual lives!

It is God who makes ...

you stand firm in Christ.

He anointed us, set his seal

of ownership on us,

and put his Spirit in our

hearts as a deposit,

guaranteeing what is to come.

—2 CORINTHIANS 1:21–22

Whatever God is doing today
in our world, he is doing through
the Holy Spirit. He has no other
agent on this planet.

When we align ourselves with the channel
of God's living grace, all kinds of
marvelous things take place. His power
energizes us to face any army, large or
small, and win victories for him.
We call upon him and he sends us
forth to accomplish what we could
never do alone, regardless of our money,
education, or track record.

No matter what difficulties confront us as believers or as local congregations, God is calling us to receive today this great promise of power as a living reality. Then in victory we will praise God alongside those believers down through the ages who have experienced for themselves the truth that "greater is he that is in you than he that is in the world"

(1 JOHN 4:4 KJV).

The church ... was strengthened;

and encouraged by the Holy Spirit, it

grew in numbers, living in the fear

of the Lord.

— A C T S   9 : 3 1

GOD GIVES POWER TO HIS CHURCH

You have been given fullness in Christ,

who is the head over

every power and authority.

— C O L O S S I A N S   2 : 1 0

CALLED TO GOD'S WORK

God nowhere asks anyone to have a large church. He only calls us to do his work, proclaiming his Word to people he loves under the anointing and power of the Holy Spirit to produce results that only he can bring about. The glory then goes to him alone—not to any denomination, local church, local pastor, or church-growth consultant. That is God's only plan.

SPEAK BOLDLY

The early Christians began dynamically in power. They were unified, prayerful, filled with the Holy Spirit, going out to do God's work in God's way and seeing results that glorified him. The hour seemed golden.

Then came the first attack. These early Christians quickly gathered a meeting of the believers and began to pray. They immediately turned to their power source.

This is how they prayed: "Sovereign Lord, you made the heaven and the earth and the sea and everything in them. … Now, Lord, consider their threats and enable your servants to speak your word with great boldness. Stretch out your hand to heal and perform miraculous signs and wonders through the name of your holy servant Jesus" (Acts 4:24, 29–30). This is the church on the move, giving us a Spirit-inspired model for today.

Isn't it strange that the group prayed for boldness? We might have expected them to pray, "Lord, help us find a safe shelter now. We need to 'lie low' for a few weeks until the heat goes away. We'll stay out of sight, and if you could just make the Sanhedrin sort of forget about us. ..."

Not at all. If anything, they prayed against backing down. They asked God to help them press on. Retreat was the furthest thing from their minds.

And how did God react?

"After they prayed, the place where they were meeting was shaken. And they were all filled with the Holy Spirit and spoke the word of God boldly" (Acts 4:31).

The first time vocalist Steve Green came to sing at the Brooklyn Tabernacle we gathered in my office with the associate pastors to pray just before the meeting began. We prayed in unison that God would come among us that day.

When we opened our eyes, Steve had an odd look on his face. "What was that vibration I just felt?" he asked. "Is there a train that runs near here, or was that really...?"

I explained that as far as I knew, the rumble wasn't caused by the power of the Holy Spirit — would to God it was! Rather, it was the passing of the "D" train in the subway that runs directly beneath our building.

For the early church that day in Jerusalem, however, the vibration was nothing short of Spirit-induced. In that prayer meeting God's power came in a fresh, new, deeper way.

These people had already been filled with the Holy Spirit on the Day of Pentecost, but here they sensed a new need. God met them with a new infusion of power. The apostles didn't claim they already had everything they needed.

Now that they were under attack, they received fresh power, fresh courage, fresh fire from the Holy Spirit.

I long more and more to be filled
with the Spirit, and to see my congregation
moved and melted under the Word,
as in great revival times, 'the place shaken
where they are assembled together,'
because the Lord has come in power.

— ANDREW BONAR

What we need today is not

cleverness or oratory—we need

messages from God's Word set

on fire by the Holy Spirit!

GOD'S PROMISE

The minute I walked in to the multiracial Brooklyn Tabernacle, I could sense that this church had big problems. The young pastor was discouraged. The meeting began on a hesitant note with just a handful of people. Several more walked in late. The worship style bordered on chaotic; there was little sense of direction. The building was in disrepair and the finances were a disaster.

After we had some Sunday night times of prayer around the altar, when people got into the habit of calling on the Lord, our attendance grew to fifty or sixty. But I knew God wanted to do much more ... and he would, if we provided good soil in which he could work. The truth is, I knew there were countless churches across the city and the nation that had not baptized a hundred truly converted sinners in a year, and most not in several years. Any growth came simply through transfers from one church to another.

New York City was a hard mission field, but transfer growth was not what God had in mind for us. What we needed instead was a fresh wind and fresh fire. We needed the Holy Spirit to transform the desperate lives of people all around us. Alcohol and heroin dominated the neighbor-hood; LSD was also a problem, and cocaine was starting its wicked rise. Prostitutes were working a couple of street corners within three blocks of the church. Urban decay had clearly set in.

I despaired at the thought that my life might slip by without seeing God show himself mightily on our behalf. My wife Carol and I didn't want merely to mark time. I longed and cried out for God to change everything—me, the church, our passion for people, our praying.

One day I told the Lord that I would rather die than merely tread water throughout my career in the ministry ... always preaching about the power of the Word and the Spirit, but never seeing it. I abhorred the thought of just having more church services. I hungered for God to break through in our lives and ministry.

Carol and I had frankly admitted to each other that unless God broke through, the Brooklyn Tabernacle was doomed. We couldn't finesse it along. We couldn't organize and market and program our way out as other churches had. The embarrassing truth was that sometimes even I didn't want to show up for a service—that's how bad it was. We had to have a visitation of the Holy Spirit, or bust.

About that time, I came down with a cough that would not go away. My in-laws became so concerned about my health that they paid my airfare to visit them in Florida. While out on a fishing boat I had time to think and pray.

"Lord, I have no idea how to be a successful pastor," I prayed softly out there on the water. "I haven't been trained. All I know is that Carol and I are working in the middle of New York City with people dying on every side, overdosing on heroin, consumed by materialism, and all the rest. If the gospel is so powerful …"

I couldn't finish the sentence. Tears choked me. Fortunately, the others on the boat were too far away to notice.

Then quietly but forcefully, in words heard not with my ear but deep within my spirit, I sensed God speaking: *If you and your wife will lead my people to pray and call upon my name, you will never lack for something fresh to preach. I will supply all the money that's needed, both for the church and for your family, and you will never have a building large enough to contain the crowds I will send in response to my people praying.*

I was overwhelmed. I knew I had heard from God. God was simply focusing on the only answer to our situation—or anybody else's for that matter. His word to me was grounded in countless promises repeated in the Scriptures; it was the very thing that had produced every revival of the Holy Spirit throughout history. It was what I already knew, but God was now drawing me out, pulling me toward an actual experience of himself and his power. He was telling me that my hunger for him and his transforming power would be satisfied as I led my tiny congregation to call out to him in prayer.

God had promised to provide, to respond to our cries for divine help. We were not alone, attempting the impossible in a heartless world. God was present, and he would act on our behalf.

Ask and it will be given to you; seek
and you will find; knock and the door
will be opened to you. For everyone
who asks receives; he who seeks finds;
and to him who knocks, the door will
be opened.

— MATTHEW 7 : 7 – 8

The key to a dynamic Christian church

is the person and work of the Holy Spirit.

Christianity is hopeless without him.

God didn't send the Holy Spirit to give us

thrills and chills; he sent the Spirit to

empower us to win lost people to Jesus.

The work of God is not by might of men
or by the power of men but by his Spirit.
It is by him the truth convicts and converts,
sanctifies and saves. The philosophies
of men fail, but the Word of God in the
demonstration of the Spirit prevails.

—SAMUEL CHADWICK

"Not by might nor by power, but by

my Spirit," says the LORD Almighty.

—ZECHARIAH 4:6

THE SPIRIT IS ESSENTIAL

The church cannot be the church without the Holy Spirit abiding and empowering it. The degree to which we understand and experience the Spirit of God will be the exact degree to which God's plan for our churches will be accomplished.

The very people who are thumping the Bible the most vigorously are often the ones trying to have a church without the Holy Spirit. They think that teaching alone can cause their members to live a "victorious Christian life"— but it can't be done without experiencing the power of the Holy Spirit. Vows and promises alone, no matter how sincere, can never overcome the power of the world, the flesh, and the devil.

Jesus said, "Here I am! I stand at the door and knock. If anyone hears my voice and opens the door, I will come in and eat with him, and he with me.

To him who overcomes, I will give the right to sit with me on my throne, just as I overcame and sat down with my Father on his throne.

He who has an ear, let him hear what the Spirit says to the churches."

—REVELATION 3:20–22

Only by the Holy Spirit can we see people as he sees them and feel their need as he does.

MOVE FORWARD

The work of God can only be carried on by the power of God. The church is a spiritual organism fighting spiritual battles. Only spiritual power can make it function as God ordained.

No matter the society or culture, the city or town, God has never lacked the power to work through available people to glorify his name.

When we sincerely turn to God, we will find that his church always moves *forward*, not *backward*. We can never back up and accommodate ourselves to what the world wants or expects. Our stance must remain militant, aggressive, bold.

INTO GOD'S WILL

In the fall of 1994, I was invited to speak
at a Christian music gathering in Indianapolis.
I arrived on a Thursday, and that evening I still
wasn't sure what I should speak about the next
morning. I was leaning toward a simple message
of encouragement—one I had preached before.
I thought it would go well in this festive setting.
I certainly didn't want to do anything contro-
versial or get in anybody's face about anything.

I went to part of the evening concert but left
around eight o'clock to return to my hotel
room. There I began to seek the Lord about
my message for the next morning. I reviewed
my sermon outline and then went to prayer.
The longer I prayed, the more this nice, familiar
sermon idea went dead inside of me.

In time I felt drawn toward the text
"My house will be called a house of prayer"
(Mark 11:17), a message I had preached not
long before at the Brooklyn Tabernacle. It's
a very direct message. It deals with Jesus'
cleaning the merchants out of the temple and
pointedly calls the audience to what the church
is really for, as opposed to all the misuses we
make of it.

I began to argue with the Lord. A sermon on cleaning merchants out of the house of God—at a music festival? Surely not! But it was getting late. I had no notes for that message anyway. I could remember only parts and pieces of what I had preached at home. Surely I wasn't going to get up in front of 10,000 people and just "wing it."

Yet the Holy Spirit seemed to persistently whisper to my heart, *This is why I brought you here. This is what I want you to preach. Are you going to do my will, or are you just going to go out there tomorrow morning and "perform"?*

I kept struggling in prayer. Finally, after an hour or two, I relented. I opened my Bible to the passage in Mark as I said, "God, help me. If you want to use this to speak to the people tomorrow morning, all right. Show me how to reconstruct this sermon."

Around midnight something very unusual happened. I was attacked by a tremendous feeling of fear and insecurity. I began to imagine the audience turning against me. Something or someone kept whispering to me that this "prophetic" message wasn't going to fit the setting at all. It seemed as if I was battling against forces intent on disrupting this message I now felt so strongly.

The sun had just come up that Friday morning. On less than four hours' sleep, I began getting ready for the day ahead. All too soon I was across the street at the arena. As the host began to introduce me, I walked out onto the stage and nervously took stock of what I was up against. *O God, help me now!* I prayed silently.

I began speaking in a soft voice. "I want to talk for a few moments about something so vital, and yet it's so simple. It's so familiar to us—and that's the danger. I want our session this morning to be something that will make a difference in our lives...."

It seemed that the longer I spoke, the more clarity came into my heart. I felt calm inside. I could sense the Holy Spirit helping me. I was just pouring out what I felt God wanted me to say. Some of the last sentences I uttered were, "God says that when you call, he will answer. The hard cases some of you are facing today— the answer won't come from another seminar. We have too many mere technicians who are only stressing methodology, and they are increasingly invading the church. The answer is not in any human methodology. The answer is in the power of the Holy Spirit. The answer is in the grace of God."

I walked off the stage. Inside I felt peace: God had indeed helped me do what he wanted in that place.

During the next few months I chatted occasionally with my friend who had invited me to speak in Indianapolis. He mentioned that the sales of that morning's video were beyond any in their previous experience. Even after two or three years, the video continued to sell and to spread all across the country by word of mouth.

More than one pastor called to say, "I don't know you personally, but I just wanted you to know that I showed your video in my first morning service—and the people got up en masse to come pray at the altar, which is not the custom in our church. When it was time for them to clear out so the next crowd could come for the next service, I didn't know what to do. The new people just came in and joined the first group in calling upon God and waiting in his presence."

Great reports kept coming back of what transpired—*all because the Lord took over my plans in a hotel room and showed me his will. I hadn't wanted to preach that message at all. But God knew exactly what he wanted me to say. It was merely the Holy Spirit coming to the aid of a human vessel who didn't really know what he was supposed to be doing. The Spirit is the one who leads us into God's will.*

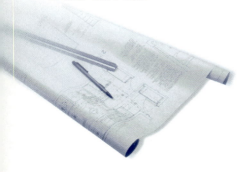

Dear Father, thank you
for your mercy and the
salvation you have given
me in Jesus Christ. Please
forgive me for all my sins
and shortcomings. Draw
me to you, and begin
a new work of grace in me.
Make me the person you
want me to be.
Fill our churches
with your fresh wind
and fresh fire.
Break our pride,
soften our hearts
and fill us to overflowing
with your Holy Spirit.
O God, do all this
so that the Name of Jesus
will be exalted
throughout the earth.
Amen.

My message and my preaching were
not with wise and persuasive words but with
a demonstration of the Spirit's power,
so that your faith might not rest
on men's wisdom, but on God's power.

−1 CORINTHIANS 2:4−5

The Spirit of the Sovereign LORD is on me,
because the LORD has anointed me
to preach good news to the poor.
He has sent me to bind up the brokenhearted,
to proclaim freedom for the captives
and release from darkness for the prisoners,
to proclaim the year of the LORD's favor.

−ISAIAH 61:1−2

The church that multiplies

committees and neglects prayer

may be fussy, noisy, enterprising,

but it labors in vain and

spends its strength for naught.

It is possible to excel in mechanics

and fail in dynamics.

There is an abundance of machinery;

what is wanting is power.

—SAMUEL CHADWICK

Christ was crucified in weakness,
yet he lives by God's power.
Likewise, we are weak in him,
yet by God's power we will live
with him to serve you.

−2 CORINTHIANS 13:4

We constantly pray for you
that our God may count you worthy
of his calling, and that by his power
he may fulfill every good purpose
of yours and every act prompted
by your faith.

−2 THESSALONIANS 1:11

Let us put ourselves under the

Holy Spirit's teaching anew,

to be taught the Word,

and how to preach the Word,

not our thoughts upon it.

One spark of lightning

is worth a thousand

tame candle flames;

so one sentence given

by the Holy Spirit is worth

volumes of any other.

—ANDREW BONAR

Only the power of the Holy Spirit

can set people free from their bondage and

energize saints for Christian service.

WAITING FOR
THE POWER

Now a lot of us type A personalities don't want to hear the instruction "Wait." We're eager to get going. But we will accomplish far more if we spend time waiting for the power of the Spirit. The work of the church needs not just the correct message concerning Jesus but also the power that Jesus promised his followers.

Jesus did not say to wait for any certain manifestation: the flickering flames, the rushing winds, or the speaking in tongues. He pointed the disciples to their need of receiving spiritual *power*. The thrust in the New Testament was always toward the power itself rather than any particular manifestations that came alongside the power. Today I am afraid that the priority sequence is reversed in some circles. People are fascinated with visible manifestations rather than real power from the Spirit to do God's work. What the New Testament believers wanted most was to receive special ability from God, and any manifestations were unexpected side issues.

Jesus gave the disciples a divine promise that has never been rescinded: "You will receive power *when* the Holy Spirit comes on you; and you *will* be my witnesses" (Acts 1:8, emphasis added). In other words, the Great Commission of evangelism is the great work of the church — and it will be done only by the power of the Holy Spirit.

CLOTHED WITH POWER

The water of God's Spirit is absolutely free, but we must wait by faith continually to receive fresh infillings of this promise from the Father. This is how Luke ends his gospel narrative as he records Jesus' last words to his disciples: "I am going to send you what my Father has promised; but stay in the city until you have been clothed with power from on high" (Luke 24:49).

Two thousand years later this is still the greatest need of the Christian church—to wait regularly in seasons of corporate and individual prayer until we are "clothed with power from on high." These are the *garments* Jesus will still give his people—supernatural ability, might, and power from the Holy Spirit so we can accomplish great things for God's glory.

We can be clothed with the very power of God himself! It is not through human talent or earthly resources that the true Christian church is built, but rather through men and women saturated with God's Spirit and full of his Word.

SPEAK WITH BOLDNESS

We must never be intimidated by what the devil tries to do whether by striking out at us as individuals, or at the local church, or at the Body of Christ as a whole. We must instead trust the Holy Spirit to give us the words to speak and to do so with boldness.

LORD, SEND A
REVIVAL AND LET IT
BEGIN IN ME, AND IN
YOUR PEOPLE
PREACHING IN YOUR
CHURCHES. BUT NO
MATTER HOW OR
WHERE IT BEGINS
LORD, SEND A
REVIVAL OF THE
HOLY SPIRIT AMONG
YOUR PEOPLE.

I pray that out of God's glorious riches he may strengthen you with power through his Spirit in your inner being, so that Christ may dwell in your hearts through faith.

— EPHESIANS 3:16–17

THE POWER
SOURCE — THE
HOLY SPIRIT

HELP FROM GOD

We Christians seldom admit that we don't know how to pray. Many of us have been taught since childhood how to put sentences together that sound like a prayer, to the point that we are professionals at it. Some can turn out an eloquent presentation to God at a moment's notice.

Prayer born of the Spirit, however, is another dimension of calling on God to the point of having the Holy Spirit supernaturally assist us. This is not a worked-up emotionalism but a powerful promise of help from God himself!

FRESH OUTPOURING
OF LOVE

If we do not yearn and pray and expect
God to stretch out his hand and do the supernatural, it will not happen.

Carol and I have found that unless God
baptizes us with fresh outpourings of love, we
would leave New York City *yesterday*! We don't
live in this crowded ill-mannered, violent city
because we like it. Whenever I counsel a guy
who has sexually abused a little girl, I'm tempted
in my flesh to throw him out of my office.
This isn't an easy place for love to flourish.

But Christ died for that man. What could
ever change him? What could ever replace the
lust and violence in his heart? He desperately
needs to be surprised by the power of a loving,
almighty God.

If the Spirit is not keeping my heart in line
with my doctrine, something crucial is missing.
I can affirm the existence of Jesus Christ all
I want, but in order to be effective, he must
come alive in my life in a way that even the
pedophile, the prostitute, and the drug pusher
can see.

THE POWER OF
THE SPIRIT

Standing six-feet-four, Willie McLean is our church's head of security and walks with me every Sunday as I move in and out of our four crowded services. What an irony that he should be serving God in this line of work, since his "rap sheet" with the NYPD is, as the saying goes, as long as your arm. If you read it, you would say Willie was absolutely hopeless, truly incorrigible—just lock him up and throw away the key.

Willie started off horribly in junior high by getting his girlfriend pregnant—the twelve-year-old daughter of a New York City cop. "I didn't know she was only twelve," he says with a shy smile. When Elise gave birth to the baby, her parents tried to keep things quiet … until the next year, when the young couple did it again!

By his junior year of high school, Willie had dropped out, preferring to spend his days in the pool rooms of Harlem or out with the street hustlers. He also began stealing cars. At age seventeen, Willie started experimenting with drugs.

"It seemed like I could not stop going to jail," Willie remembers. "I kept getting ninety days for this, sixty days for that: writing 'numbers' ... trespassing ... disorderly conduct ... shoplifting from Macy's. It seemed like the streets just kept calling my name." Eventually, twenty-one counts of armed robbery led to a ten-year sentence.

When Willie finally got out of prison in 1976, Elise and the two children were amazingly still waiting for him. The couple got married at last, over the strong protest of her family. But the angry, twenty-seven-year-old Willie was still out of control.

After the death of a daughter from diabetes, Willie became all the more violent. He stole $20,000 in drugs from a supplier, sold them, and used the money to enter the prostitution business. Soon, however, the cash flow could not keep up with his expenses. Before long, the drug supplier figured out who the culprit was and put out a contract on Willie's life. Willie was making a call at a public phone booth one day when, all of a sudden, bullets started flying. Willie twisted in first one direction and then the other as a 9mm bullet bounced off the phone and into his face. Passing through his tongue, the bullet split his jaw. Meanwhile, another bullet entered his shoulder from the back.

Lying on the street, watching his blood run toward the gutter, Willie prayed for one of the few times in his life: "God, please don't let me go out like this."

When Elise, who had recently started attending our church, came to visit him in the hospital this time, she just stared. She showed no emotion at all.

"Aren't you going to cry?" Willie asked.

"No, I'm gonna pray for you. You need Jesus bad…."

But Willie McLean was not yet ready to change. He met another girlfriend named Brigitte, who bore him two more children in the coming years. Brigitte's incensed mother tried to have him killed as well, but Willie managed to charm the designated gunmen into leaving him alone.

He did not fare so well with the police in Jamaica, Queens, however, after they photographed him from a rooftop making a drug sale. The sentence this time was a year on Rikers Island plus five years of probation. And that was the point when Elise finally managed to get her thirty-nine-year-old husband to our church.

"The choir began singing that day," he recalls, "and I just opened up. My nose started running, and then I was actually crying!"

Before Willie knew it, an invitation to come to Christ began. At the front of the church he spread out his arms and cried, "O God—I just can't take it anymore. I can't go on…."

Today Willie explains in his soft-spoken voice, "The Lord didn't just save me — he delivered me. He mended my marriage. He gave back my self-esteem. God has turned my life inside out. He has blessed me and my family incredibly."

The power of the Holy Spirit captured this giant of a man and stopped his self-destruction. And the same Spirit of God who turned Willie McLean to Christ and salvation has kept him clean and victorious ever since. Think of the power potential we have available to us through God's Word anointed by the Holy Spirit. Not just the Word only, nor an emphasis solely on the Spirit — we must have together the Word and the Spirit bringing blessing and salvation.

The Spirit is here on the earth, waiting to

respond to our longing for him to come in

fresh power upon us.

God has a good many children
who have just barely got life but no power
for service. The Holy Spirit coming
upon them with power is distinct
and separate from conversion.
I believe we should accomplish more
in one week than we should in years
if we had only his fresh baptism.

A great many think because
they have been filled once, they are going
to be full for all time after; but O my friends,
we are leaky vessels and have to be kept
right under the fountain all the time in order
to keep full. Let us keep near Him.

—D.L. MOODY

"I will pour water on the thirsty land,
and streams on the dry ground;
I will pour out my Spirit on your offspring,
and my blessing on your descendants.
They will spring up like grass in a meadow,
like poplar trees by flowing streams.
says the Lord.

–ISAIAH 44:3–4

If you ... know how to give good gifts
to your children how much more
will your Father in heaven give
the Holy Spirit to those who ask him!

–LUKE 11:13

Thank God that the Holy Spirit
is accessible wherever you are.

I have been thinking of prayer
particularly of praying for the Holy Spirit
and its descent. It seems to me I have always
limited God in this request. I have now felt
that I might rationally ask for the
influence of the Spirit to come down
not only on individuals but on a whole people,
region, country and world. On Sa
I set myself to do this and the
was very angry with me yesterday
I am now convinced it is my duty
privilege and the duty of every other
Christian to pray for as much of
Holy Spirit as came down on the
of Pentecost, and a great deal more
I know not why we may not ask for the
entire and utmost influence of the
Spirit to come down, and asking
see the full answer.

—DANIEL NASH

A PRAYER WARRIOR

About two years ago, I took my seat among the Prayer Band members of the church and asked five or six of them to pray for me. I opened my heart to the Lord as they gently laid hands on my shoulders.

After a while, I heard a female voice among them intercede for me. As the woman led out in prayer, I discerned that her whole heart was in it and that the Holy Spirit was helping her. Her prayer was fervent, bold and scriptural. She quoted promise after promise from God's Word. As she continued in prayer, she began asking the Lord to help and strengthen me in areas that no one could know about but God and me. She seemed to read right into my heart and life as she pleaded, asking God to help this frail man who was her pastor. I wept openly as she led us to the throne of heaven, where God so readily provides his mercy and grace.

Who is this woman who prays with such spiritual insight and faith? I wondered. I didn't recognize her voice, and I never looked around to see who she was. During subsequent weeks, however, the same thing happened two more times. A group around me was praying when suddenly

that same voice interceded. It was as if she could not be denied. I don't know all the members of the Prayer Band personally, but I finally discovered who God was using to bless me— a tall, slender African-American woman in her mid-thirties. Her name is Silvia Glover.

You might be wondering what kind of spiritual roots a prayer warrior like Silvia must have. Which Bible seminary did she attend? Is she a former missionary who learned how to pray effectually and fervently after many years of dedicated ministry? How many years of Sunday school and church services does it take to carve out a woman who is so mighty in prayer? If your back was against the wall, trust me, you would want Silvia Glover in your corner to call out to heaven. But where did this woman come from, and how did she become the prayer warrior she is today?

Silvia came from a wild background and a chaotic life filled with verbal abuse, violence, alcohol, drugs, and stealing. At age twelve she was partying and drinking beer; at fourteen she was "doing the clubs." Her alcohol and marijuana consumption increased. By age twenty she joined a group who were Rastafarians (members of a religious sect originating in Jamaica) and drug dealers. The Rastafarians believed that getting high was the way to get closer to God. But Silvia was totally insecure and battled severe depression and thoughts of suicide.

One day while visiting Brooklyn Tabernacle, Silvia yielded herself wholeheartedly to the things of God. She was willing to do anything and go anywhere for her new Master.

Who else but Jesus Christ could embrace such a chaotic life and transform it into a life of virtue and spiritual excellence? I was overwhelmed with thanksgiving when I learned the life story of this prayer warrior who daily holds Carol and me up to God in prayer.

Although Silvia speaks well publicly,
her real ministry is that of prayer—
as witnessed during those Tuesday nights
at the Brooklyn Tabernacle. It is a
shame so many churches no longer seek
or appreciate this spiritual gifting
from God. A heart that prays and a
church that gives itself to communion
with the Lord—these are two of the
great secrets that bring God's blessing
in untold ways upon the earth.

A PASSION FOR THE SPIRIT

God will manifest himself in direct proportion to our passion for him. The principle he laid down long ago is still true: "You will seek me and find me when you seek me with all your heart" (Jeremiah 29:13).

O GOD, SPLIT THE HEAVENS AND COME DOWN! MANIFEST YOURSELF SOMEHOW. DO WHAT ONLY YOU CAN DO.

THE SPIRIT IS FREE

Just as there is no salvation without Jesus, there can be no Christian living and witness without the Holy Spirit.

Oh, how we need to wake up to the fact that the Holy Spirit's blessing and power is the key to everything.

And here is the best news: *It's all free!* Salvation is free. The forgiveness of sin is free. A reservation in heaven is free. And the power of the Holy Spirit to live the Christian life is free, too. Everything we need is free from the hand of a gracious God. He waits now to come and meet every need in your life and mine.

"You will seek me and find me when you seek me with all your heart. I will be found by you," declares the Lord.

–JEREMIAH 29:13–14

God rewards those who earnestly seek him.

–HEBREWS 11:6

From one man God made every nation of men, that they should inhabit the whole earth; and he determined the times set for them and the exact places where they should live. God did this so that men would seek him and perhaps reach out for him and find him, though he is not far from each one of us.

–ACTS 17:26–27

The old saying is true:
If you emphasize only
the Word, you dry up.
If you emphasize only
the Spirit, you blow up.
But if you hold on
to both, you grow up.

The Spirit of God first imparts love;
He next inspires hope;
and then He gives liberty.

—D.L. MOODY

Praise the Lord.
How good it is to sing praises to our God,
how pleasant and fitting to praise him! ...
He heals the brokenhearted
and binds up their wounds.
He determines the number of the stars
and calls them each by name.
Great is our Lord and mighty in power;
his understanding has no limit.

—PSALM 147:1, 3–5

We have put our hope in the living God,
who is the Savior of all men, and especially of
those who believe.

—1 TIMOTHY 4:10

"I will pour out my Spirit on all people,"
says the Lord.

—ACTS 2:17

The Holy Spirit dwelling in the hearts of believers would conquer the age-old dilemma of "I want to be different but can't. I know what's wrong—but I keep doing it anyway." This empowerment by the Spirit is the dynamic source throughout time for all who live and labor for Jesus Christ.

GOD'S EQUATION

God has given us a very simple equation if only we have the faith to reach out and experience it:

The Holy Spirit's power is our greatest need.

This power and blessing is freely promised to all God's people.

This promise can only be fully received through sincere praying in faith and through waiting on God for his blessing to come.

This is what happened in the New Testament, and this is the only thing that will satisfy our souls' thirst.

God's work in the world is usually
a joint project: he works with us as
we yield ourselves to work with him.

POWER OVER EVIL

Marissa Cunningham is a polished and articulate attorney who is bright, intelligent, and capable. About five years ago, while still in law school, Marissa found herself at loose ends due to some reversals in her life. Casting a shadow over her future road toward graduation were her divorce, the stress of raising her daughter alone, and especially, her inability to find a summer internship.

Marissa felt empty. Soon a vague sense of spiritual gloom settled over her. At times the horrible thought of ending her life would tantalize her. Clouds of depression blocked out any rays of light from her soul.

One day while walking along Fourth Avenue in Brooklyn, she saw a familiar sign on a storefront: BONTANICA. She knew this was a fortune-telling parlor based on Santeria, a form of Caribbean witchcraft. She walked in and the *curandero* invited her to sit down. Before long, he was telling her a number of specific events from her past.

He identified one of her friends by name and said this person had performed black magic against Marissa. And, of course, he would be willing to help reverse the curse for a price.

He told her that if she would come back on Friday with ninety dollars in cash, he would lead her through a cleansing ritual. They would take a chicken, rub it against Marissa's body "to get the scent," and then kill it. Draining the blood, he would take the animal to a cemetery for burial. This he assured her would be the answer she needed. But Marissa was repulsed by the idea. Still, she thought, if this would really solve her problem and free her spirits, perhaps she should go along.

In the past Marissa had visited our church, so now in her uncertainty she decided to stop by our office. "I need to speak with a pastor — someone with a lot of power!" she insisted. Elsie Lherisson, a member of our staff who just "happened" to have grown up in Haiti and knew all about Santeria, began telling Marissa that the goodness of God was much stronger than her personal distress and that God alone had the power to deliver her. She invited Marissa to come to our Foundation Bible Study class that evening.

By the end of the night, Marissa felt that these people truly cared about her. They didn't treat her as if she was a nut for going to a fortune-teller; they wanted to give her a better answer. "God is good and he wants good things for you," someone said. "You don't have to kill a chicken to solve your problem. The truth is the necessary blood was already spilled—two thousand years ago when Jesus died on the cross for you. He loves you, he cares about you, and he can set you free." Then Marissa prayed a sincere prayer for forgiveness and cleansing, and stepped from darkness into light.

On Tuesday night, she returned to the prayer meeting. When I invited people to come forward for special prayer, she responded. "I just knew God loved me and was reaching out for me," she remembers.

We discipled Marissa in the subsequent months. Today she is a solid believer and a wonderful asset to our church.

Gospel work in our day must be more than just little stories, doctrinal presentations and polite lectures. It must carry a sense of God's living power. It must show a living Holy Spirit who is still active on the earth. We hear endlessly about the growing menace of the occult and Satan's hold on people. But if Satan is alive and working in the earth, can we not expect the living, all-powerful Spirit of God to work also? The antidote to satanic schemes is twofold: the Word of God and a demonstration of Holy Spirit power.

Nothing about God will change. Tomorrow he will be no more anxious to help our lives, our families, and our churches than he is right now. If we simply avail ourselves of his promises, we will see him do things we could never ask or think, just as he did in the New Testament. It is time to press on.

I pray that out of his glorious riches
God may strengthen you with power through his
Spirit in your inner being, so that Christ may
dwell in your hearts through faith. And I pray that
you, being rooted and established in love,
may have power, together with all the saints,
to grasp how wide and long and high and deep
is the love of Christ, and to know this love that
surpasses knowledge — that you may be filled
to the measure of all the fullness of God.

Now to him who is able to do immeasurably
more than all we ask or imagine, according to his
power that is at work within us, to him be glory
in the church and in Christ Jesus throughout all
generations, for ever and ever! Amen.

— EPHESIANS 3:16–21

HEAVENLY FATHER,
I PRAISE YOU FOR ALL THE
GRACE AND MERCY YOU
HAVE SHOWN ME IN THE
PAST. TEACH ME TO PRAY
MORE AND TRUST IN YOU
WITH ALL MY HEART.
GIVE ME THE KIND OF
FAITH THAT WILL WAIT
PATIENTLY FOR THE
FULFILLMENT OF YOUR
PROMISES. HELP ME TO
HUMBLE MYSELF BEFORE
YOU AND LISTEN CAREFULLY
TO YOUR WORD.
MAKE ME A HOLY AND
COMPASSIONATE PERSON
SO THAT OTHERS CAN SEE
JESUS IN MY LIFE.
I WANT MY HEART TO BE
YOUR SPECIAL HOME.
IN CHRIST'S NAME, AMEN.